Developing Literacy
SENTENCE LEVEL

SENTENCE-LEVEL ACTIVITIES FOR THE LITERACY HOUR

year

Christine Moorcroft

Series consultant:

Ray Barker

A & C BLACK

Reprinted 1999, 2000, 2001, 2002 (twice)
Published 1999 by
A&C Black Publishers Limited
37 Soho Square, London W1D 3QZ
www.acblack.com

ISBN O-7136-5172-5

The author and publisher would like to thank Ray Barker and
the following teachers for their advice in producing this
series of books: Tracy Adam; Hardip Channa; Lydia Hunt;
Madeleine Madden; Helen Mason; Judith Metcalfe; Heather Morrealy;
Yvonne Newman; Hilary Walden; Fleur Whatley; Annette Wilson.

A CIP catalogue record for this book is
available from the British Library.

A & C Black uses paper produced with elemental chlorine-free pulp,
harvested from managed sustainable forests

Printed in Great Britain by
St Edmundsbury Press Ltd, Bury St Edmunds, Suffolk.

Contents

Introduction

Developing Literacy: Sentence Level supports the teaching of reading and writing by providing a series of activities to develop children's understanding that grammar is about the way in which we combine words in sentences in order that the reader can understand what we have written: that writing must make sense to the reader as well as to the writer. To understand grammar, children need to know about the different types of words which make up sentences.

The children learn to examine the effect of their choice of words and to question whether it communicates what they intend. They find out how their choice affects the audience. They also investigate the effect of changing the words in a sentence. They learn about the importance of devices which stress certain words (and their effects on the reader) and that punctuation is a set of marks used to make sentences easier to read: it shows variation which would otherwise only be possible in speech.

The activities are designed to be carried out in the time allocated to independent work during the Literacy Hour. They support the objectives of the National Literacy Strategy *Framework for Teaching* at sentence level and incorporate strategies which encourage independent learning – for example, ways in which children can check their own work or that of a partner. Investigation is given greater emphasis as the series progresses towards **Year 6**.

Year 4 helps children to develop:

- an understanding of elements of grammar introduced in Years R, 1, 2 and 3 and –

    how to take account of grammar and punctuation when reading aloud;
    the function of verbs in sentences, verbs with similar meanings and the most appropriate one to use;
    the relationship between tense and the purpose and structure of a text and how to form the present, past and future tenses;
    the function of adjectives and adjectival phrases in sentences;
    the ways in which adjectives can be changed to form comparatives and superlatives, words which can be used with them to intensify them and the way in which adjectives of a similar type can be arranged in order of intensity;
    the function of adverbs in sentences and their relationship to verbs;
    agreement between verbs and their subjects;
    the ways in which some words can be changed for particular purposes, such as the changing of verb endings, and of the endings of adjectives to form their comparatives and superlatives.

- an understanding of sentence-construction and punctuation introduced in Years R,1, 2 and 3 and –

    commas for separating and enclosing units of a sentence;
    the use of apostrophes to indicate possession, and the contractions of words;
    the ways in which clauses can be separated, enclosed and joined;
    the purposes of colons, semi-colons, dashes and hyphens;
    the effects of changing the order of the words in a sentence, both to keep the same meaning and to alter the meaning;
    statements, questions and orders;
    the structure of arguments.

Year 4 also encourages the children to investigate. For example, they investigate the effect on the meaning of a sentence when words are moved about (for example, changing *I see what I eat* to *I eat what I see*) and they explore the formation of hyphenated words.

Words from the high-frequency lists in the National Literacy Strategy *Framework for Teaching* are incorporated and the activities include different genres of text.

The following logos are used to remind the children to use dictionaries and thesauruses:

Extension

Most of the activity sheets end with a challenge (**Now try this!**) which reinforces and extends the children's learning and provides the teacher with an opportunity for assessment. These more challenging activities might be appropriate for only a few children; it is not expected that the whole class should complete them. On some pages there is space for the children to complete the extension activities, but others will require a notebook or separate sheet of paper.

Organisation

For many of the activities it will be useful to have available scissors, glue, word-banks, a variety of dictionaries and fiction and non-fiction texts. To help teachers to select appropriate learning experiences for their pupils, the activities are grouped into sections. The pages do not require to be presented in the order in which they appear in the books, unless otherwise stated.

Teachers' notes

Brief notes are provided at the bottom of most pages. They give ideas and suggestions for making the most of the activity sheet. They sometimes make suggestions for the whole-class introduction, for the plenary session or, possibly, for follow-up work using an adapted version of the activity sheet. These notes could be masked before copying.

Structure of the Literacy Hour

The following chart shows an example of the way in which an activity from this book can be used to achieve the required organisation of the Literacy Hour.

Clauses (page 38)

Whole class introduction   15 min

Read a shared text which has sentences with different numbers of clauses. The children can identify the beginnings and endings of sentences and then the verbs. Once they have found the verbs, ask them how many clauses each sentence has (each clause has a verb) and to indicate each clause. They could explore the effect on their reading of splitting the sentences into their individual clauses. Draw their attention to any words which are omitted when they do this: which type of word are they? (They are likely to be connectives.)

Whole class activity   15 min

Play 'human sentences'; each child is given a large piece of paper on which is written a clause which either begins or ends a sentence, or a connective word. Choose a child who has the beginning of a sentence and ask him or her to hold it up for the others to see. Ask who has a clause which could end the sentence and, finally, who has a word to join the clauses. They have to arrange themselves in the correct order for the rest of the class to read the sentence.

Group work   20 min

The children work from a text in which they have to find and copy specific clauses (decided by the teacher): for example, a clause about the weather, a clause about the main character's feelings, and so on.

Independent work   20 min

The others work independently from **Clauses** (page 38, **Developing Literacy: Sentence Level Year 4**).

Whole class plenary session   10 min

The children could explain how they recognise a clause and how they know where it begins and where it ends. They could contribute to a set of 'instructions for finding clauses' which could be refined through discussion and displayed so that they can use it during later work to help them to recognise clauses.

Using the activity sheets

Grammatical awareness

This section provides activities which develop the children's grammatical awareness by drawing attention to the different types of words and their roles in a sentence: nouns, verbs, adjectives (including comparatives and superlatives, and adjectival phrases), personal pronouns, possessive pronouns, connectives and adverbs. It shows the children how to make the possessive forms of nouns and consolidates their understanding of those terms, and it develops their understanding of the use of the past tense and of the correct forms of verbs in the future tense.

Find the mistake (page 9) revises agreement between nouns, pronouns and verbs. The children have to identify the words in each sentence which are wrong, and put them right. Talk about the words which need to be changed, removed or added, encouraging the children to say whether they are nouns, pronouns or verbs.

Verb fun (page 10) revises verbs. Some children might be able to make up other examples of verbs with a missing letter for a partner to solve. **Verb vases** (page 11) revises the use of verbs with similar meanings. The children could use the examples provided as the basis for a class 'verb thesaurus' (arranged in alphabetical order) to which they can add as they come across interesting verbs. **Verb power** (page 12) encourages the children to think about the verbs they use and to find the one which is the most apt (see also **Developing Literacy: Word Level Year 4**).

Into the future (page 13) introduces the future tense in a way which focuses the children's attention on changes made to verbs when their tenses are changed, and on the use of *will* and *shall*. **Tense time** (page 14) shows which tenses are used in different texts and why. In **Tense change** (page 15) the children explore the ways in which verbs are altered when sentences are changed from one tense to another.

Adverbs (page 16) asks the children to explore the use of adverbs, to explain how they are used and with which words they are associated. Ask the children to notice the endings of adverbs. All those in the examples end in 'ly', but the children should be cautioned not to think that any word which ends in 'ly' is an adverb; they could look for words with 'ly' endings which are not adverbs: for example, lively, homely and curly (adjectives). They could also look for adverbs which do not end in 'ly'. **Adverb quiz** (page 17) provides consolidation of the children's understanding that an adverb adds information about a verb, by drawing their attention to the word 'how' (for example, 'How did they sing?', 'How did he speak?') **Adverb animals** (page 18) introduces interesting adverbs which the children can use in their own writing. There are no 'right answers', but the following are suggested: I slither slyly/slily, I purr contentedly, I bark bravely, I roar raucously, I sing sweetly, I sprint swiftly, I step steadily, I march majestically, I hoot hauntingly, I swim playfully. **Adverb files** (page 19) shows the types of information an adverb can give about a verb. In the extension activity, extra adverbs which the children could add to the files include: (sound) quietly, softly; (speed) quickly, hurriedly, rapidly; (light) radiantly, vividly; (feelings) proudly, angrily; (character) kindly, helpfully, meanly; (strength) faintly, powerfully. **Adverbs alike** (page 20) encourages the children to think about adverbs which have similar meanings and which they can use in their writing. **Adverb menu** (page 21) shows how adverbs can be made from adjectives (see also **Developing Literacy: Word Level Year 4** which introduces the use of suffixes for changing words from one part of speech to another). **Difficult adverbs** (page 22) encourages the children to approach difficult words by first working out what type of words they are from the rest of the text. **'Not' adjectives** (page 23) is about adjectival phrases (see pages 28 and 29). The children consider alternatives for adjectival phrases which include 'not'. This links with word-level work on prefixes (for example, unwell, unhealthy, uninteresting) and antonyms (for example, well/ill, fresh/stale, interesting/boring). There are several alternative answers for some of the examples: 1) not nice = nice/pleasant 2) not clean = dirty/unclean 3) not tall = short 4) not easy = difficult/hard 5) not smooth = rough/bumpy 6) not well = unwell/ill/sick/poorly 7) not healthy = unhealthy 8) not right = wrong 9) not polite = impolite/rude 10) not interesting = uninteresting/boring 11) not sharp = blunt 12) not fresh = stale. **Adjective search** (page 24) revises adjectives while focusing on those which have similar meanings and the consideration of the most suitable adjective for the purpose.

Pronoun chart, Pronoun happy families and **Pronoun happy family cards** (pages 25-27) revise pronouns.

Phrases (page 28) introduces phrases which are easy to spot in a sentence. Groups could play 'Consequences': they write the 'who or what' phrase at the top of a long strip of paper, fold it over and pass it to the next person, who writes a verb phrase (what the subject did, does or will do), folds it over and then passes it to the next person, who writes an adverbial phrase (where, how, when or why the subject did the action). **Adjectival phrases** (page 29) introduces adjectival phrases as groups of words which act as one word – an adjective. They could look for adjectival phrases in poetry as well as in fiction and non-fiction texts, and point out the nouns which they describe. **House for sale** (page 30) asks children to identify adjectives and adjectival phrases. The extension activity encourages the children to consider alternative adjectives for particular contexts. It is linked with word-level work on synonyms and antonyms and encourages the children to explore the ways in which they can vary the adjectives they use in their writing, whether they want the same meaning or a different shade of meaning. **Comparing** (page 31) introduces the terms 'absolute', 'comparative' and 'superlative' and begins with examples which are formed by simply adding 'er' and 'est'. This links with word-level work on the changes which have to be made to the ends of words before suffixes are added. Some children will need help with the irregular examples such as 'bad' and 'good'. They could investigate the comparatives and superlatives of long adjectives, whose endings do not change, such as beautiful, wonderful and attractive (instead they take *more* and *most*). **Adjective arrows** (page 32) introduces scales of intensity for adjectives with similar meanings. It builds on the children's developing vocabulary of groups of adjectives (see **Developing Literacy: Sentence Level Year 3**). **Adjective staircase** (page 33) introduces words which can be added to an adjective to show its intensity.

Word webs (page 34) shows how words can be changed to make them into different parts of speech. It is linked with word-level work on changing the endings of words before adding suffixes. The children could also investigate words which can be different parts of speech without alteration: for example, care, rest, run and nest (nouns or verbs), and warm (adjective and verb).

Invented words (page 35) revises nouns, verbs, adjectives and adverbs. With a partner, the children could play a game in which they use an invented word (or a real word used in a different way from its normal usage and as a different part of speech). The partner asks questions which can be answered 'Yes' or 'No' to find out what the word means: A. I *triangle* every Saturday. B. Do you *triangle* at home? A. No. B. Is *triangling* a sport? A. Yes. B. Do you have special *triangling* clothes? A. Yes. B. Is *triangling* swimming? A. Yes.

Sentence-construction and punctuation

In **Comma sandwiches** (page 36) the children learn that commas can be used to surround a phrase as well as to separate parts of a sentence or items in a list. Encourage them to look for sentences in their own writing to which they can add a phrase in this way. **Misplaced commas** (page 37) revises commas and can be used for assessment.

Clauses (page 38) revises connectives and introduces clauses. Point out the changes which must be made to the sentences before combining them as clauses of one sentence. **Find the clauses** (page 39) develops the children's ability to recognise clauses. Ask them to describe the changes they make when they split a sentence into two separate sentences.

Meet the colon (page 39) shows how a colon can be used to separate two units of a sentence. The main uses of colons are to introduce an identifier or an example (or examples). The children could investigate the difference between lists which are preceded by a colon and those which are not. Ask them to explain how they know when a colon is needed in a sentence. **Meet the semi-colon** (page 41) introduces the semi-colon and revises clauses. The children could compare the ways in which clauses are combined with connectives (page 38) and semi-colons. They could also compare the use of semi-colons and colons. **Punctuation game** (pages 42–43) revises full stops, question marks, exclamation marks, colons, semi-colons and commas. The children can glue their sentences into a book or folder for editing later and for the teacher to assess their learning. Encourage them to check their punctuation by reading the sentences aloud. **Make a dash** (page 44) shows how dashes (sometimes called 'en dashes' or 'en rules') can separate parts of a sentence. They are used in a similar way to commas, but a dash is a much stronger separator than a comma, semi-colon or colon. The children could explore and discuss the substitution of dashes for commas, colons or semi-colons. Encourage them to use whichever feels better in the sentences they write. **Two into one** (page 45) introduces the hyphen. The children might find some words which are hyphenated in the dictionary but not in everyday use, such as chess-board, bird-song and barn-owl. They could add words to make other hyphenated words from those provided: for example, multi-purpose, right-handed, long-sighted and tongue-tied. In **Star words** (page 46) the children develop their understanding of hyphenated words: they consider which part of speech they are and, in the extension activity, work out the part of speech of the individual words which make them up (to do this they should try the words out in sentences). **Air-blue and wave-whitened** (page 47) links with text-level writing; it encourages children to explore the sounds of hyphenated words and their use in poetry. Answers: *after-storm-lit* – bright after the darkness of a storm; *air-blue* – clear blue, like the sky; *Eden-green* – green like a leafy garden (the Garden of Eden); *Heaven-haven* (safe haven or harbour); *leaf-crowned* – covered with leaves; *years deep dust* – dust which has been gathering for years; *pity-pleading eyes* – eyes which are pleading for mercy or pity; *memory-traces* – almost-forgotten memories; *silver-scaled fish* – fish with shiny scales which look like silver; *wave-whitened* – with colour washed out by the sea.

The owner's apostrophe (page 48) introduces the use of the apostrophe to make the possessive form of a noun. It can be linked to work on possessive pronouns, which do not have apostrophes. The children might find it interesting that the apostrophe in the possessive form of a noun indicates missing letters, now out of use (Dad's car = Dad his car); this shows that the two uses of the apostrophe are, in fact, the same! (See pages 51 and 52). **Apostrophes in titles** (page 49) revises the use of capital letters in titles while consolidating the children's understanding of the apostrophe to indicate belonging. **The owners' apostrophes** (page 50) develops the children's ability to use apostrophes; here they form the possessive forms of plural nouns, including irregular ones. **Contractions 1** (page 51) introduces the use of the apostrophe in contractions and shows the complete forms of commonly contracted words and that an apostrophe represents missing letters. The children could look for contractions in books and other texts and notice which genres of text use them and which do not. **Contractions 2** (page 52) develops the understanding of contractions; it introduces the irregular contractions, *shan't* and *won't* which have no apostrophe to indicate the omission of 'll'; *won't* also has 'o' substituted for 'i'. The children can look for examples of the contraction for 'of' in phrases such as *will o' the wisp, cat o' nine tails* and *leg o' mutton*.

What did they say? (page 53) revises punctuation marks and alternative words for 'said' and 'asked'.

In **The same but different** (page 54) the children turn sentences around, keeping their meaning the same but improving the way in which they are written. They could share the changes they make to their own writing and make suggestions for improving one another's writing. **Positive and negative** (pages 55) encourages the children to investigate the changes which are made when a positive sentence is made negative. They might need reminding that negatives are not the same as opposites. **Statements and questions** (page 56) encourages investigation of the ways in which a statement is changed when it becomes a question. **That's an order!** (page 57) encourages the investigation of the ways in which a statement is changed when it becomes an order, and vice versa, by writing orders in the imperative form of the verb. The term 'imperative' could be introduced. **Silly sentences** (page 58) shows the way in which the words at the beginning of a sentence govern the others. It invites the children to explore the changing of sentences in a way which makes their meaning nonsense, although they are still grammatically correct. In **Sentence pairs** (pages 59–60) the children investigate the changing of the word-order of a sentence to give another grammatically correct and logical sentence, but with a different meaning. **An argument** (page 61) is about the kind of information which is needed for an argument. It introduces useful words for argument-writing. Other information which could be invented and provided for the extension activity includes: the cost of repairing the school and a report about the other schools to which the children would have to go. The children could also consider how they would feel if they had to change schools and how it would affect their parents and their teachers. **Agreement** (page 62) introduces the term 'subject' (of a verb) and develops the children's ability to check and correct the agreement of verbs with their subjects. **Proof-reading: 1 and 2** (pages 63–64) revise punctuation, including capital letters. They introduce the terms 'lower-case' and 'upper-case' as well as proof-reading marks, which provide a neat way for correcting work.

Glossary of terms used

abbreviation A shortened form. Sometimes an apostrophe is used to denote letters which are omitted; for example, *can't*.

absolute The basic form of an adjective which has not been altered to form the comparative or superlative.

adjective A word which describes (qualifies) a noun; for example, *big*, *sweet* and *soft*.

adjectival phrase A phrase which acts as an adjective; for example, The dog *with the long ears*.

adverb A word which qualifies a verb; for example, *sadly*, *quickly*.

adverbial phrase A phrase which acts as an adverb; for example, He slept *in his chair*, She walked *up the hill*.

agreement The way in which linked words agree with one another in terms of person, gender, singular or plural, and tense.

antonym A word which has the opposite meaning to another.

apostrophe (') A punctuation mark which denotes the omission of a letter or letters, and the possessive form of a noun (which is, in fact, a contraction of a defunct combination of the noun and possessive pronoun: *Jim's = Jim his*).

clause A group of words which is a distinct part of a sentence and can act as a sentence. A clause includes a verb.

colon (:) A punctuation mark mainly used to introduce a list or an identification (information which is needed to answer a question raised by the first part of the sentence; for example, *We saw three kinds of tree: an oak, an elm and a rowan*.

comma (,) A punctuation mark which is used to separate or surround parts of a sentence and items in a list.

comparative A form of an adjective used in comparison: *bigger, smaller, longer*.

conjunction A word used to link sentences or clauses or to connect words within the same phrase; for example, *and*, *but*.

connective A word (or phrase) which makes a connection between one phrase, clause, sentence or paragraph and another. A connective can be a conjunction or an adverb, a prepositional expression or a pronoun.

contraction A shortened form (using an apostrophe to denote omitted letters) of a word or words; for example, *don't*.

dash (–) A punctuation mark, sometimes called an 'en dash' or an 'en rule', used to separate or enclose a phrase or clause.

exclamation A word or sentence which expresses emotion such as surprise, shock, pain, pleasure, anger, fear or humour.

exclamation mark (!) A punctuation mark used after an exclamation.

genre A specific type of writing or other medium of communication; for example, legend, newspaper story or poem.

hyphen (-) A punctuation mark used to link two words so that they act as one.

object The recipient of an action; for example, Mum read the *newspaper*.

order A sentence which gives an instruction; for example, *Keep off the grass*.

person A text may be written in the first person: for example, (singular) *I went, I am*, (plural) *we went, we are*; the second person: for example, (singular and plural) *you went, you are*; or the third person: for example, (singular) *he/she/it went, he/she/it is*, (plural) *they went, they are*.

personal pronoun (see **pronoun**).

phrase A group of words which act as a unit; for example, the old man went to sleep *in his chair* (see also **adjectival phrase** and **adverbial phrase**).

possessive pronoun (see **pronoun**).

possessive The form of a noun which shows ownership: *Jane's, the girl's, the children's, the boys'*.

prefix An affix at the beginning of a word which changes the word's meaning; for example, *undo, replay, overcome*.

pronoun A word used instead of a noun, for example: (personal pronouns) *I, you, he, she, it, we, they*; (dependent possessive pronouns) *my, your, her, his, its, our, their*; (independent possessive pronouns) *mine, yours, his, hers, its, ours, theirs*.

semi-colon (;) A punctuation mark used to separate clauses of equal importance in a sentence.

statement A sentence which gives information; for example, *He likes reading*.

subject The subject of a verb is the person or thing which does it: for example, *Mum* read the newspaper.

suffix An affix at the end of a root word; for example, *singing, slowly*.

superlative A form of an adjective used in comparison: *biggest, smallest, longest*.

synonym A word with the same meaning as another.

tense The tense of a verb shows when it happens: for example, (present) she *writes*/she is *writing*, (past) she *wrote*/she *has written*, (future) *she will write*.

title The name of a book, play, poem, etc, but also part of a person's name; for example, *Mr, Mrs, Miss* and *Ms*. A person's title always begins with a capital letter. Mr and Mrs are abbreviations of Mister and Mistress (which has become corrupted to Missus or Missis). Ms is a modern abbreviation of a woman's title (Mrs and/or Miss), by analogy with Mr.

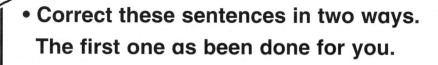

Find the mistake

• **Correct these sentences in two ways.**
  The first one as been done for you.

Look at the verbs, nouns and pronouns.

1. | The boys asks if there is any glue left. |

The boys ask if there is any glue left.

The boy asks if there is any glue left.

2. | She begin to cry. |

3. | It am cold. |

4. | The men read his book. |

5. | Mice is rodents. |

6. | Clare and James does her homework. |

Now try this!

• **Write three different sentences which contain nouns, verbs and pronouns from the chart.**

You can also use 'a' and 'the'!

Nouns		Verbs		Pronouns	
girls	car	buy	chase	she	it
mum	horses	eat	ride	them	his
shoes	grass	grow	drive	her	he

Teachers' note Model the first example with the children: ask them which word is wrong and what is wrong with it. In the extension activity, remind the children they can change the verb endings.

Developing Literacy
Sentence Level Year 4
© A & C Black 1999

9

Verb fun

Each of the verbs in these sentences has a letter missing.

- Underline the verbs.
- Write the sentences correctly.

The roses row beautifully.

The musician pays and we all lap.

Watch out - the jellyfish might sing if you read on it!

The teacher raised Amy because she had tied hard.

The spider pins a web and flies tick to it.

She sows off because she can sell 'multiplication'.

- **Correct the verbs in these sentences:**

Oil the water and arm the teapot.

He is saying in Cardiff but he lies in Swansea.

Teachers' note The children might need some practice in spotting missing letters. Write verbs to which they can add a letter to make other verbs; for example, rust (trust), rap (wrap), stop (stoop). The children could compile lists of such verbs.

Developing Literacy
Sentence Level Year 4
© A & C Black 1999

10

Verb vases

- **Write a verb in each flower which has a similar meaning to the words in the vase.**
- **Write two more verbs in each vase.**

The verbs in each vase have similar meanings.

jump

hop
vault
bound

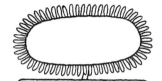

notice
observe
spy

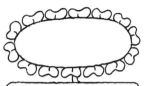

grate
graze
scrape

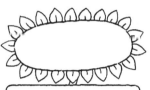

snatch
steal
grasp

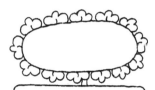

shuffle
hobble
tiptoe

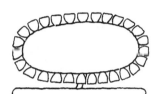

yell
bawl
bellow

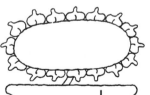

scrawl
inscribe
print

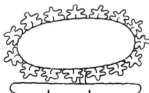

slumber
doze
nap

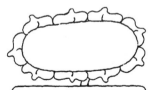

mumble
whisper
declare

Now try this!

- **Write lists of verbs which mean**

throw   cook   find

Use a thesaurus.

Teachers' note Talk about the meaning of 'similar' and how it differs from 'the same'. Different groups of children could write sentences using all the verbs from a vase. They could substitute the verb in each sentence with a different verb from the same vase and compare the effects of each verb.

Developing Literacy
Sentence Level Year 4
© A & C Black 1999

Verb power

• **Write six sentences which say what is happening in the picture.**

Use interesting verbs.

Example: 'A police car <u>sped</u> past' is more interesting than 'a police car <u>went</u> past'.

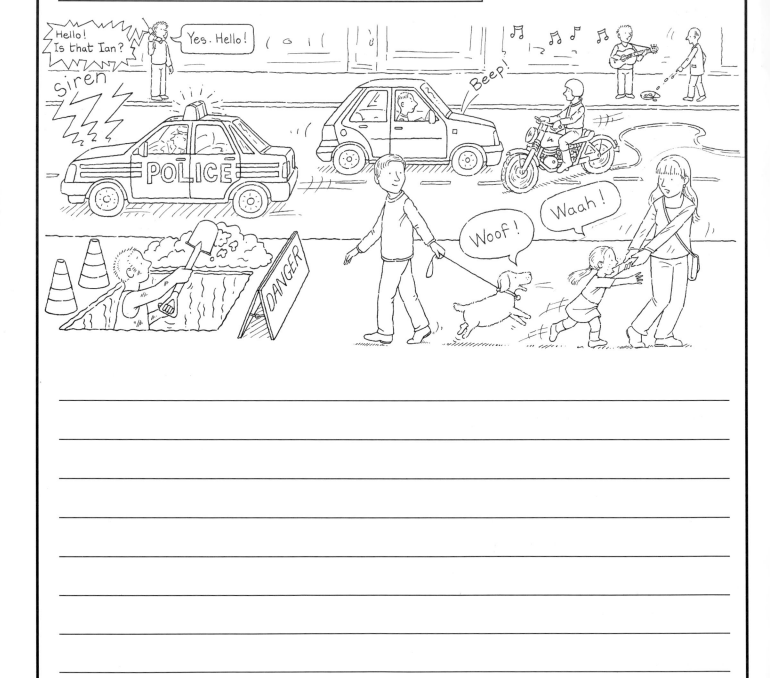

_____

_____

_____

_____

_____

_____

_____

• **Re-write the sentences, using different verbs.**

Teachers' note To introduce the activity, discuss interesting verbs which could be used to describe what is happening in the picture. During the plenary session the children could read aloud, and compare, the descriptions they have written. List all the verbs they used.

**Developing Literacy
Sentence Level Year 4**
© A & C Black 1999

Into the future

- **Verbs in the future tense have** `shall` **or** `will`.

I shall	I shall write	we shall	we shall write
you will	you will write	you will	you will write
he, she, it will	he/she/it will write	they will	they will write

- **Read the sentences.** • **Write them in the future tense.**
- **In the time machine, write the words which you changed or added.**
  The first one has been done for you.

Present	 Time machine	**Future**
Simon goes to Spain on holiday.	will go	Simon will go to Spain on holiday.
You have a new reading book.		
I sing in the bath.		
Ella drives a train.		
The mouse is hiding from the cat.		
We are working hard.		
They watch television every day.		

Now try this!

- **Write these sentences in the future tense.**
It is a fine day. The sun is shining and a gentle breeze is blowing. It is dry and warm.

Teachers' note To introduce the activity, ask a child to write a sentence about something he or she, has done, is doing now and will do/is going to do. Underline the verbs and talk about their tenses. Ask other children to re-write the sentences in different tenses.

Developing Literacy
Sentence Level Year 4
© A & C Black 1999

Tense time

- **Underline the verbs in each text.**
- **Write the tense in the box underneath.**

I <u>had</u> lunch at twelve o'clock.

past

A cold front will move across Ireland. It will bring sleet and snow. Winds will be light and northerly.

Carrot soup

carrots   vegetable stock
1 chopped onion   1 teasp. ginger
Cook the onions until soft. Add the chopped carrots, ginger and stock. Bring the mixture to the boil and simmer for 30 minutes.

He opened the door into the garden. The moon was bright. He could see the path clearly.

Hotel Bella
This modern hotel has a terrace which overlooks the beach. There are three restaurants.

You will meet a tall, dark stranger.

Sand martins nest in burrows which they dig in river-banks.

Some of the soldiers were on horseback. They had bows and arrows, axes and swords.

Now try this!

- **Copy the chart.**
- **List other kinds of texts which are written in each tense.**

Past	Present	Future
stories	instructions	weather forecasts

Teachers' note Read extracts from shared texts in different tenses. Ask the children in what tense they would expect the following to be written, and why: a prediction, a history book, a report, a story and instructions.

Developing Literacy
Sentence Level Year 4
© A & C Black 1999

Tense change

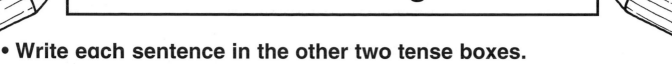

• **Write each sentence in the other two tense boxes.**

Past

1. I left my key at home.

2. _____

3. _____

4. The children wrote stories and drew pictures.

Present

1. _I leave my key at home._

2. She is eating a pizza and drinking lemonade.

3. _____

4. _____

Future

1. _____

2. _____

3. We shall stay at a hotel in Paris.

4. _____

Now try this!

• **Write three sentences in the future tense. Let a partner change them to the past and the present.**

Teachers' note Read a shared text and invite the children to change it to the other tenses, a sentence at a time, and to notice which words they change, add or omit.

Developing Literacy
Sentence Level Year 4
© A & C Black 1999

Adverbs

The underlined words are adverbs.

He shouted <u>loudly</u>.

The dog barked <u>angrily</u>.

Remember, 'shouted' and 'barked' are verbs.

- **What do adverbs do?** _____

_____

- **Underline the adverb in these sentences.**
- **Which word does the adverb describe?**
- **Write the word in the box.**

1. Nirmal writes neatly.

2. The sun shone brightly.

3. He suddenly jumped to his feet.

4. She laughed cheerfully and skipped along the path.

5. Emma gently stroked the cat.

6. The man timidly opened the door and looked around.

7. The waiter briskly whisked the cloth off the table.

8. Tom whistled tunefully while he washed the dishes.

Now try this!

- **Write an alphabetical list of adverbs.**

Include as many letters of the alphabet as you can.

Example: angrily, badly, carefully...

Teachers' note Read the examples with the children and ask them to point out the adverbs in a shared text. Can they explain what adverbs do: what do they tell the reader? They should notice that adverbs are connected with verbs.

Developing Literacy
Sentence Level Year 4
© A & C Black 1999

Adverb quiz

• **Answer each question with an adverb.**

 How did they sing?   Sweetly

 How did he speak?

 How did Kate dance?

 How did Tony play?

 How did the woman whisper?

 How did the snail creep?

 How did she weep?

 How did the boy whisper?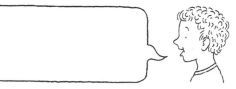

 Now try this!

• **Write some 'adverb questions' for a partner to answer.**

Teachers' note Play a game in which someone demonstrates an action, and the others have to name the verb and say how it is done; for example, 'She sat down heavily', 'He whistled softly'.

Developing Literacy
Sentence Level Year 4
© A & C Black 1999

Adverb animals

- **Read what the animals say.**
- **Add an adverb to each sentence.**

I slither _____.

I purr _____.

I roar _____.

I bark _____.

I sing _____.

I sprint _____.

I march _____.

I step _____.

I hoot _____.

I swim _____.

- **Write sentences about six of the animals. Use different adverbs.**

Now try this!

Use a thesaurus.

Teachers' note There are no 'right answers', but some answers are more appropriate than others. Read and discuss the meanings of the adverbs with the children; they should read the entire page before they begin. Point out the alternative spellings of 'slyly'/'slily'.

Developing Literacy
Sentence Level Year 4
© A & C Black 1999

Adverb files

Adverbs can say different kinds of things about verbs.

• **Write the adverbs in the correct files.**

Adverbs

slowly	sturdily	suddenly	dimly	lazily
bravely	deafeningly	dishonestly	noisily	brilliantly
dreamily	honestly	fairly	sadly	loudly
weakly	feebly	eagerly	swiftly	happily
darkly	brightly	speedily	excitedly	silently

Sound

Speed

Light

Feelings

Character

Strength

Now try this!

• **Write two other adverbs in each file.**
• **Use an adverb from each file in a sentence.**

Use a thesaurus.

Teachers' note The children could collect examples of adverbs from books, and either add them to the files on this page, or start new files: for example, adverbs which describe how neatly something is done or how politely someone acts.

Developing Literacy
Sentence Level Year 4
© A & C Black 1999

Adverbs alike

- Write the adverbs under the headings which have a similar meaning.

Adverbs

cruelly
cleverly
boldly
foolishly
silently
miserably
fearlessly
soundlessly
savagely
sensibly
roughly
noiselessly
senselessly
courageously
brainlessly
unhappily
intelligently
woefully

wisely

stupidly

sadly

bravely

quietly

fiercely

Use a thesaurus.

- Collect adverbs under other headings, for example:

Now try this!

neatly

truly

gently

Teachers' note Afterwards, the children could write sentences using an adverb from one set. Then they could substitute other adverbs from the set and decide which is the most appropriate.

Developing Literacy
Sentence Level Year 4
© A & C Black 1999

Adverb menu

• **In each gap write an adverb made from the word in the box.**

Starters

Orange Surprise

Segments of orange [warm] _____ spiced with

ginger, [dainty] _____ floating in a sea of

raspberry sauce.

Golden vegetable soup

Fresh garden vegetables [smooth] _____ blended

and [light] _____ seasoned with garlic and pepper.

Main Courses

Sunset baked potatoes

Baked potatoes with a filling of [perfect] _____

mashed potato and tuna [delicate] ___ ___ flavoured

with parsley.

Fish feast

[Fresh] _____ caught plaice with [crisp] ___

fried potato chips.

Desserts

Home-made ice cream

[Loving] _____ blended cream with eggs, sugar

and vanilla.

Lemon clouds

Light-as-air meringues [gentle] _____ resting

on a bed of lemon custard.

• **Write sentences using the adverbs in the menu.**

Teachers' note Read menus as shared texts and ask the children to point out the adverbs and the verbs they describe. Ask them why adverbs are used in menus. They could read the menus aloud, omitting the adverbs and discussing the effect of this.

Developing Literacy
Sentence Level Year 4
© A & C Black 1999

Difficult adverbs

Each sentence contains an adverb.
The adverb might be difficult to read.
You might not know what it means.

Use a dictionary.

- Underline each adverb.
- Circle the verb which it describes.

1. The man stared sombrely at everyone.

2. She smiled amiably at the children.

3. The waves tossed tempestuously on to the shore.

4. He gave orders imperiously.

5. The cat dozed serenely in the shade of the tree.

6. Simon answered the questions candidly.

7. Mari drove the car capably.

8. The editor checked the text meticulously.

9. Mum cautiously climbed the ladder.

10. The burglar alarm rang ceaselessly.

Now try this!

- **Write what you think each of the adverbs means.**
- **Look up the meanings and make a note of them.**
- **Write four other sentences which contain difficult adverbs.**

Teachers' note Model the first example with the children; they should recognise the adverb even if they can not read it.

Developing Literacy
Sentence Level Year 4
© A & C Black 1999

22

'Not' adjectives

- **Replace 'not' and the adjective with another adjective.**

The meaning of the sentence should not change.

Example: That is <u>not good</u>. That is <u>bad</u>.

1. | His words were not nice.

2. | The room is not clean.

3. | She was not tall.

4. | That is not an easy task.

5. | It was not a smooth ride.

6. | She is not well.

7. | The plant did not look healthy.

8. | That is not right.

9. | It is not polite to push.

10. | The book is not interesting.

11. | The pencil was not sharp.

12. | The loaf is not fresh.

Now try this!

- **Write six other 'not' adjective sentences for a partner to re-write with a different adjective.**

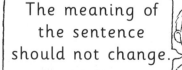

The meaning of the sentence should not change.

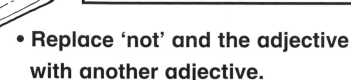

Teachers' note The children could also look in books for sentences in which an adjective can be replaced by 'not' with a different adjective.

Developing Literacy
Sentence Level Year 4
© A & C Black 1999

Adjective search

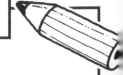

There are ten adjectives in the wordsearch.
Each of them has a similar meaning to one of the
adjectives on the easel.

- Mark each adjective in the word search.
- Write it on the easel underneath the one with
  a similar meaning.

g	b	s	k	l	p	m	l	y	v	d	e
m	e	r	r	y	g	r	y	z	i	i	s
a	u	j	v	r	n	o	q	r	c	s	i
t	l	y	u	t	x	h	w	s	i	m	m
s	o	l	i	d	k	z	p	v	o	a	p
f	u	r	i	o	u	s	b	d	u	l	l
g	o	i	e	n	v	i	o	u	s	t	e
c	o	u	r	t	e	o	u	s	j	y	b
p	l	e	a	s	a	n	t	s	m	d	o
f	o	o	l	i	s	h	r	n	e	f	z

1. easy

_____

2. cruel

_____

3. nice

_____

4. gloomy

_____

5. jealous

_____

6. polite

_____

7. firm

_____

8. stupid

_____

9. cheerful

_____

10. angry

Now try this !

- **Make adverbs from each of
  the adjectives on the easel.**

Remember the rule
for making adverbs
from adjectives
ending in ⌐y⌐.

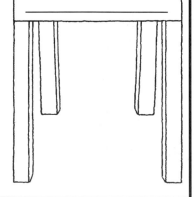

Teachers' note The adjectives in these examples could be used to begin a class 'adjective thesaurus', perhaps organised in a ring-binder to allow pages to be added, on which the children can write new adjectives as they come across them.

Developing Literacy
Sentence Level Year 4
© A & C Black 1999

Pronoun chart

• **Complete the pronoun chart. Write the pronouns you would use for each person.**

The first person singular has been completed for you.

Examples

		I	me	my	mine	myself
Singular	1st person	I				
	2nd person					
	3rd person					
Plural	1st person					
	2nd person					
	3rd person					

Examples:
- ____ can sing.
- The rain soaked ____.
- The sun hurt ____ eyes.
- The food is ____.
- all by ____ self / ____ selves

Now try this!

• Write sentences using

we	us
our	ours
ourselves	

Teachers' note Revise the term 'person': point to yourself and say 'I am the first person'; stand next to another child, and say 'We are the first person'; say to another 'You are the second person', and so on. Write the pronouns.

Developing Literacy
Sentence Level Year 4
© A & C Black 1999

Pronoun happy families

• **Deal five cards each, face down.**

• **Put the spare cards face down on the table (Pile A).**

3 or 4 players

<u>How to play</u>

The player on the left of the dealer goes first, then the next on the left, and so on.

• **On your turn, try to make a set of pronouns for a person. If you can, put it face up on the table.**

Some sets have more cards than others. Look at your chart (page 25).

Examples:

1. | I | me | my | mine | myself |

2. | it | its | itself |

• **Pick up a card from Pile A to replace each one in your set.**

• **If you can not make a set, put one card on the table, face down (Pile B) and take one from Pile A.**

• **When Pile A has been used up, shuffle Pile B and use it as Pile A. Start a new Pile B.**

• **When all the cards have been used up, score one point for each card in your sets. The winner is the player with the highest score.**

Teachers' note The children should first complete page 25. Provide them with the cards from page 27. Encourage them to read and follow the instructions on this page. Note that some persons have more pronouns than others. Continued on page 27.

Developing Literacy
Sentence Level Year 4
© A & C Black 1999

Pronoun happy family cards

	I	me	my
mine	myself	you	your
yours	yourself	he	him
his	himself	she	her
hers	herself	it	its
itself	we	us	our
ours	ourselves	yourselves	they
them	their	theirs	themselves

Teachers' note Photocopy the page and glue it on to card. Laminate it before the children cut out the cards, both to strengthen the cards and to make them easier to handle.

Developing Literacy
Sentence Level Year 4
© A & C Black 1999

Phrases

A sentence contains groups of words which belong together.
These groups of words are called <u>phrases</u>.
A phrase does not make sense on its own.

Example:

The great boulder	rolled slowly	down the hill.
Phrase 1	**Phrase 2**	**Phrase 3**

• Write phrases to complete these sentences:

Who or what?	What did he, she or it do?	Where, how, when or why?
The red car	stopped suddenly	
A big crowd		at the football match.
	sobbed bitterly	because she was lost.
	did his homework	before he went to bed.
The teacher		
	wrote a letter	
		because he was ill.

• **Split these sentences into phrases:**

The grey cat stretched lazily on the carpet.
Three blind mice ran after the farmer's wife last night.

Teachers' note Model examples of simple sentences like those in the activity and split them into phrases. The children could make a similar chart and use it to write funny (but grammatically correct) sentences.

Developing Literacy
Sentence Level Year 4
© A & C Black 1999

Adjectival phrases

Sometimes a phrase can act as an adjective. It describes a noun or pronoun. It is called an **adjectival phrase**.

Example: He bought the dog with the sad eyes.

with the sad eyes **describes the dog.**

• **Draw lines to link the nouns to adjectival phrases which describe them.**

a fir tree

with the broken arm

a coat

filled with cheese

with the crumpled horn

without any milk

the cow

the woman

covered with snow

coffee

a baked potato

with the flowery hat

the girl

all tattered and torn

• **Write sentences using all the nouns with their adjectival phrases.**

Now try this!

• **Write four other adjectival phrases.**

Teachers' note Read shared texts such as menus which have descriptions of the dishes in which the children can look for adjectival phrases such as 'covered with', 'filled with' and 'floating in'.

Developing Literacy
Sentence Level Year 4
© A & C Black 1999

House for sale

- **Read this description of a house for sale.**
- **Underline the adjectives in red and adjectival phrases in blue.**

This is a modern, detached house with a spacious, well-stocked garden. It has a new roof. The large living room has an attractive stone fireplace and the wide patio doors lead into a delightful corner of the garden. An elegant oak staircase leads to the landing. The main bedroom has a well-made wardrobe. The whole property is clean and attractive.

Now try this!

- **Write about a car for sale, and then re-write it, with a partner, using different adjectives and adjectival phrases.**

Teachers' note Read estate agents' descriptions of homes for sale as shared texts in which the children can identify adjectives and adjectival phrases. For fun, they can re-write them in a way which puts off potential buyers.

Developing Literacy
Sentence Level Year 4
© A & C Black 1999

Comparing

- **Adjectives can be used for comparing things.**

My nose is **long**.

This is called the **absolute**.

My nose is **longer**.

This is called the **comparative**.

My nose is the **longest**.

This is called the **superlative**.

- **Write the comparative and superlative of each adjective.**

tall

quick

slow

flat

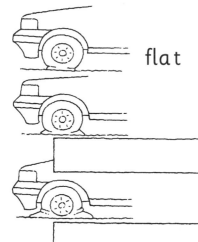

bright

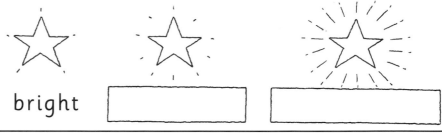

- **Write the comparative and superlative of:**
long, short, big, light, strong, weak, high, low, small, good, bad, far.

Now try this!

- **For two of the pictures, write three sentences using the adjective in the absolute, the comparative and the superlative.**

Teachers' note The children could compile tables of adjectives in their absolute, comparative and superlative forms, or contribute to a word-processed table which puts the words in alphabetical order and re-organises them as new ones are added.

Developing Literacy
Sentence Level Year 4
© A & C Black 1999

Adjective arrows

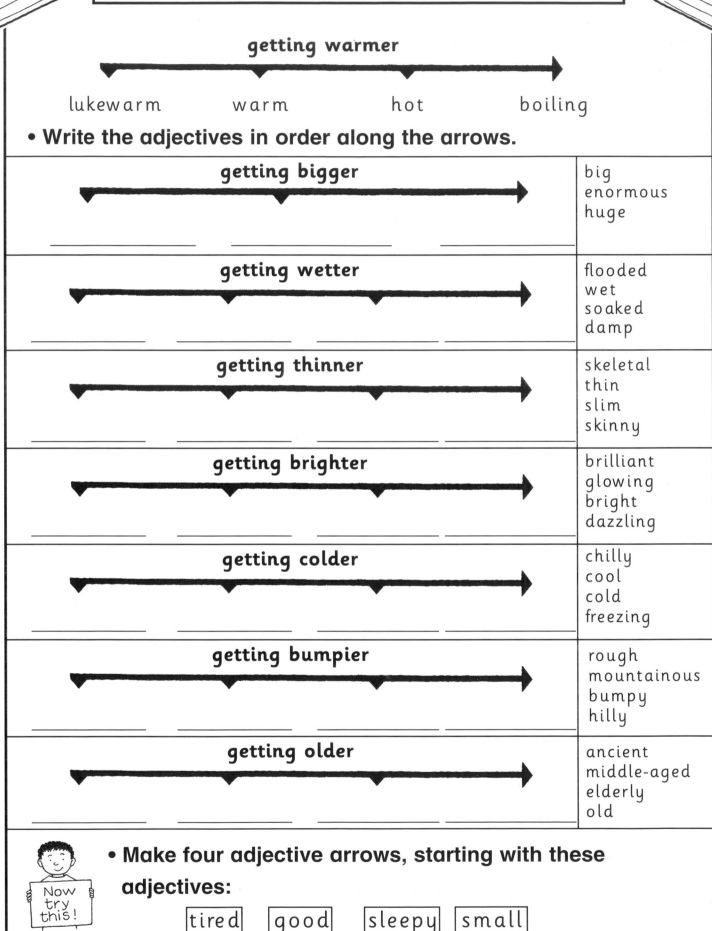

getting warmer

lukewarm   warm   hot   boiling

• **Write the adjectives in order along the arrows.**

getting bigger	big enormous huge

getting wetter	flooded wet soaked damp

getting thinner	skeletal thin slim skinny

getting brighter	brilliant glowing bright dazzling

getting colder	chilly cool cold freezing

getting bumpier	rough mountainous bumpy hilly

getting older	ancient middle-aged elderly old

Now try this!

• **Make four adjective arrows, starting with these adjectives:**

tired   good   sleepy   small

Teachers' note Ask the children to use the adjectives in each set in sentences to encourage them to think about the slight differences in meaning between them.

Developing Literacy
Sentence Level Year 4
© A & C Black 1999

Adjective staircases

- **Read the words which make the adjective stronger or weaker.**

| extremely cold |

| very cold |

cold

| quite cold |

stronger →

| slightly cold |

← **weaker**

- **Complete the adjective staircases.**

Word-bank

a little	very	slightly	amazingly
rather	a bit	incredibly	quite
fairly	exceedingly	unbelievably	extremely
really	somewhat	fantastically	enormously

heavy

long

tall

bright

- **Write sentences using two of the adjectives at the four different strengths.**

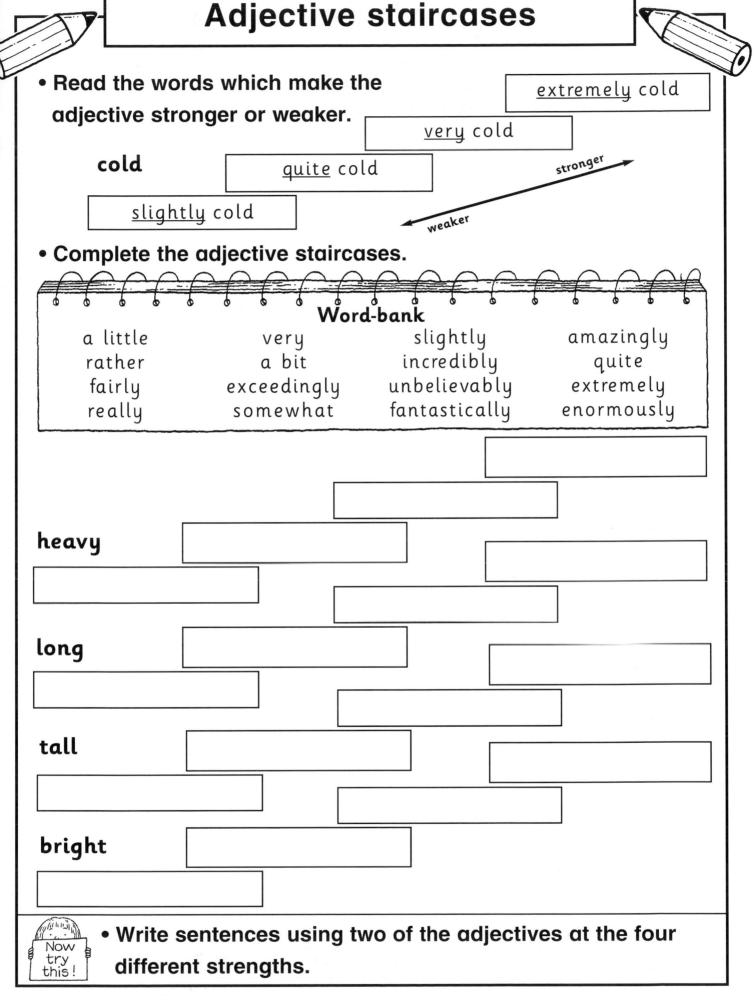

Teachers' note The children might be able to think of other (including colloquial) words to use with adjectives to alter their intensity: for example, super, mega and hyper or they could add the suffix '-ish' to them. They could make their own adjective staircases for other adjectives.

Developing Literacy
Sentence Level Year 4
© A & C Black 1999

Word webs

- Make different types of words from the adjectives.
  The first one has been done for you.

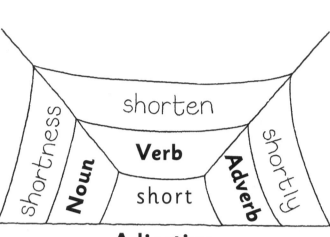

Shortness **Noun** **Verb** shorten short **Adverb** shortly

Adjective

length **Noun** **Verb** long **Adverb**

Adjective

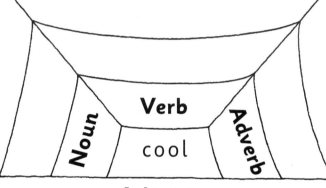

Noun **Verb** cool **Adverb**

Adjective

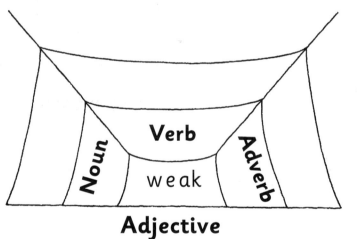

Noun **Verb** weak **Adverb**

Adjective

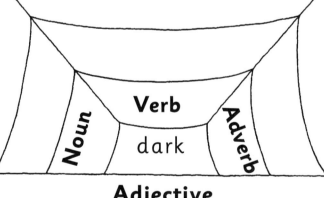

Noun **Verb** dark **Adverb**

Adjective

Now try this !

- Copy and complete the chart.

Adjective	Noun	Verb	Adverb
strong			
bright			

- Add six other adverbs to the chart.

Teachers' note Use the completed example to show the children strategies for checking which part of speech a word is: (noun) put 'the' in front of it; (verb) put 'to' in front of it or add verb endings such as 'ing' and 's'; (adverb) use it to describe a verb; (adjective) use it to describe a noun.

Developing Literacy
Sentence Level Year 4
© A & C Black 1999

Invented words

Each sentence contains an invented word.
It does not mean anything, but you can work out what
type of word it is.

• **Tick the box to show the type of word.**

	Noun	Verb	Adjective	Adverb
1. The baby cried because she lost her ungle.				
2. "I will drittle that tomorrow," she said.				
3. The weather was frush.				
4. The children leshed in the garden.				
5. She worked mardly until playtime.				
6. We saw two crunks in the park.				
7. He chose the trazest sweet.				
8. Run as slootly as you can.				

• **Write sentences, making the invented word into a real word.**

1. _____

2. _____

3. _____

4. _____

5. _____

6. _____

7. _____

8. _____

• **Invent words with a partner and use them in sentences.**

Teachers' note The children could also try replacing the invented word with a real word which makes sense, and deciding which part of speech it is: for example, 'The baby cried because she lost her rattle' (noun).

**Developing Literacy
Sentence Level Year 4
© A & C Black 1999**

35

Comma sandwiches

A phrase which adds extra information to a sentence can be surrounded by commas. The sentence makes sense without it.

Example: An old tree trunk **,** ⟨covered in moss⟩ **,** lay at the bottom of the garden.

- **Choose a phrase to add to each of these sentences.**

Surround the phrase with commas.

Phrases

mother of many children

fast asleep

looking silly

sobbing bitterly

a crafty animal

the husband of Cinderella

1. An old woman _____ used to live in that shoe.

2. Under a haystack _____ lay Little Boy Blue.

3. The wolf _____ planned to eat Red Riding Hood.

4. On the wall _____ sat Humpty Dumpty.

5. Prince Charming _____ was an expert on glass slippers.

6. Baby Bear _____ pointed to his broken chair.

Now try this!

- **Write sentences which include these phrases:**

  | higher than the clouds | | over the rainbow |

Teachers' note Encourage the children to explore the effect of removing, from a sentence copied from a book, a phrase surrounded by commas, to see if the sentence still makes sense.

Developing Literacy
Sentence Level Year 4
© A & C Black 1999

Misplaced commas

The *Daily Trumpet* was printed in a hurry.

No one noticed that the commas were in the wrong places.

• Use a red pen to mark the text where the commas should be.

The first one has been done for you.

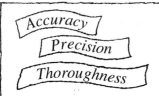

DAILY TRUMPET
ONLY 30p

SOCK SNATCHER CAUGHT

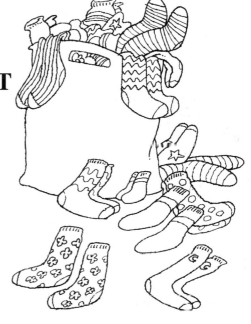

Residents of Lowton Highton and Middleton can now take their shoes off in safety. After an all-night vigil police, arrested James, Foot 74 outside, an all-night supermarket in River Street. He was carrying a, large brown leather, bag stuffed with socks. He was going on, holiday he said and, the bag contained his clothes. Inspector B. Quick never, one to miss a, clue asked him for how long he was going away. He was suspicious when Foot answered "A, week." He knew that no one however, smelly his feet needed, 476 pairs of socks for one week. Meanwhile on, the opposite side of River Street thieves, emptied the vaults of the Topland Bank.

Now try this!

• **Read the corrected text aloud for a partner to listen for the commas.**

Teachers' note The children could take turns in their groups to read out a sentence from the text in the way in which it is punctuated. Having decided where the comma(s) should be, they could read out the corrected version, to check it.

**Developing Literacy
Sentence Level Year 4
© A & C Black 1999**

Clauses

A <u>clause</u> is a group of words which can be used either as a sentence or part of a sentence. A clause contains a verb.

Example: | We <u>ran</u> down the path | | because we <u>were</u> late. |

Each sentence has one clause.
- **Join them to make two-clause sentences.**
- **Underline the verb in each clause.**

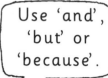
Use 'and', 'but' or 'because'.

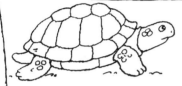

The hare mocked the tortoise. He was slow.

<u>The hare <u>mocked</u> the tortoise because he <u>was</u> slow.</u>

The hare could run like the wind. The tortoise wanted a race with him.

_____

_____

The hare laughed. He would race the tortoise.

_____

The day of the race came. They set off together.

_____

The hare stopped for a sleep. He was well ahead.

_____

The tortoise plodded on. The hare overslept.

_____

Now try this!

- **Write two one-clause sentences to say what happened when the hare awoke. Make them into a two-clause sentence.**

Underline the verbs.

Teachers' note Before the children begin this activity they might need to revise connectives; ask them to identify the connectives which join the clauses in the sentences.

**Developing Literacy
Sentence Level Year 4
© A & C Black 1999**

Commas can be used to separate the clauses in a sentence.

• **Read the passage and draw lines to separate the clauses.**

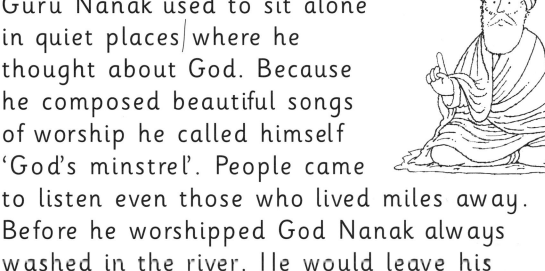

Guru Nanak used to sit alone in quiet places/where he thought about God. Because he composed beautiful songs of worship he called himself 'God's minstrel'. People came to listen even those who lived miles away. Before he worshipped God Nanak always washed in the river. He would leave his clothes on the river bank where Mardana looked after them.

One day Nanak was under the water for a long time which worried Mardana. Although Mardana and others searched the river they could not find Nanak. Mardana was overcome with grief and he sat on the river bank for three days. He had given up hope by the fourth day when out of the river walked Nanak. Everyone rejoiced but Nanak could not talk about what had happened.

Now try this!

• **List the words which join the clauses.**
The first one is 'where'.

Teachers' note The children should first complete page 38. They could also underline the verb in each clause. They could put commas in the passage where they are needed.

Meet the colon

A <u>colon</u> separates two parts of a sentence. It can be followed by essential information or a list.

A colon

| You have a choice of two fruits | : | oranges and plums. |

 What kind of fruit?

Pssst! Look!

• **Complete the messages on the notice-board using colons.**

The shop is open two days a week
_____
_____

Meet in the gym on Monday at 4pm to sign up for these sports_____
_____

The following pupils have been chosen for the Five-a-Side Football Team
_____
_____
_____

Save water
_____
_____

The chess club has a problem
_____
_____
_____

Goods are needed for the Bring and Buy Sale _____
_____

 Now try this!

• **Write four other sentences which contain colons.**

Teachers' note Discuss the example sentence: can the children say which section of it is a phrase and which is a clause? They could analyse their own sentences in the same way and investigate the use of colons in leaflets and instructions.

Developing Literacy
Sentence Level Year 4
© A & C Black 1999

Meet the semi-colon

A <u>semi-colon</u> is used to separate two clauses without a connective (like 'and' or 'but').

 These clauses could also be used as sentences.

 A semi-colon

my dad plays tennis | her best friend had moved house
it stole the sausages | he must have left it on the bus
she wanted my book | she won
I have only one | she cycled instead
it had run out of petrol | his mind was not on his game

• **Complete each sentence with a semi-colon and a clause from the note pad.**

Use full stops and exclamation marks.

1. Serena was sad _____

2. The baby did not want her rattle _____

3. James has two cats _____

4. Mum did not drive to work _____

5. Roop had lost his money _____

6. Dan played badly _____

7. The car would not start _____

8. The dog was naughty _____

9. My mum plays squash _____

10. Sara enjoyed the game _____

 Now try this!

• **Write four other sentences which contain semi-colons.**

Teachers' note Ask the children how they can check that the parts of the sentence which are separated by the semi-colon are clauses (they could look for the verbs).

**Developing Literacy
Sentence Level Year 4
© A & C Black 1999**

Punctuation game

- **Cut out the sentence strips.**
- **Take turns to pick up a sentence strip and read it.**
- **Roll the 'punctuation die' twice. If your sentence needs one (or both) of the punctuation marks shown on the die, copy it into the correct place; if not, wait until your next turn.**
- **When your sentence has all its punctuation, pick up another strip. The winner is the player with the most sentences.**

You will need a 'punctuation die'.

sticky labels

die or cube

| . | ? | ! | : | ; | , |

You can only count correctly punctuated sentences.

This is what I want to know where is my key

That is not a leopard it is a jaguar

Come and see I have found a snake

The dancers all dressed in white glided on to the stage

At the supermarket we bought milk eggs tea and a cake

Dad has a problem he has lost his wallet

Teachers' note The children should first complete pages 36-41; they might also need to revise full stops, question marks and exclamation marks. Encourage them to read and follow the instructions. Continued on page 43.

**Developing Literacy
Sentence Level Year 4
© A & C Black 1999**

Beside the river in a clump of rushes we saw it

Although she was only four she could count to a hundred

Is this your book Thomas

Mum looked everywhere but she could not find the ring

We saw three types of tree an oak an elm and a rowan

Sam chose fish and chips Ian chose a pizza

Leah wanted to join in the game but she was too shy

The inspector had a mystery to solve who stole the tarts

We need household goods cutlery crockery pans bedding and towels

They have three cars a jeep an estate car and a hatchback

May I come in or is the shop closing

We waded across the stream found the path and climbed the hill

Teachers' note Ask the children to take turns to read out their completed sentences according to their punctuation, and explain what each punctuation mark is for. If others have different ideas for the punctuation, they can explain them.

Developing Literacy
Sentence Level Year 4
© A & C Black 1999

Make a dash

A **dash** is sometimes used instead of a
comma to separate parts of a sentence.

Example: She could smell something sweet — like toffee.

A dash

• **Copy the two parts of each sentence and separate
them with a dash.**

I'm going to buy marbles

dozens of them.

She wore a new dress

a red one.

We saw two seals

the first we had ever seen.

She found her necklace

she did not know she had lost it.

The party is on Monday

or it might be on Tuesday.

Now
try
this!

• **Write six sentences containing dashes.**
• **Separate them and give them to a partner to put
back together.**

Teachers' note The children could display some of the sentences they write, together with
alternative punctuation for them such as commas or colons.

Developing Literacy
Sentence Level Year 4
© A & C Black 1999

Two into one

A <u>hyphen</u> is shorter than a dash. It is used for joining two words so that they act as one word.

A hyphen

• **Make words which have hyphens.**

left fortune
non trouble so
old
three all blue
bird
tongue semi
round
long short
colour

teller detached
sighted legged faced
tailed
purpose table blind
twister
eyed called
handed stop fashioned
maker

Begin with one of my words. End with one of my words.

_____ _____

_____ _____

_____ _____

_____ _____

_____ _____

_____ _____

• **Use six of the Twords in sentences.**

Teachers' note The children could begin a word-bank of hyphenated words. They could also have fun making up some of their own using combinations of nouns, verbs and adjectives. To simplify the activity, some of the words can be masked before copying the page.

Developing Literacy
Sentence Level Year 4
© A & C Black 1999

Star words

• **Write the hyphenated words in the correct stars.**

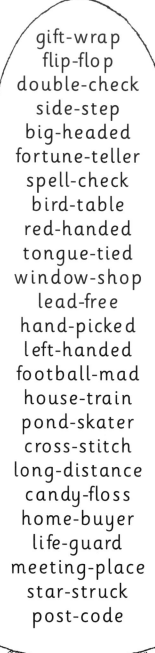

Nouns

gift-wrap
flip-flop
double-check
side-step
big-headed
fortune-teller
spell-check
bird-table
red-handed
tongue-tied
window-shop
lead-free
hand-picked
left-handed
football-mad
house-train
pond-skater
cross-stitch
long-distance
candy-floss
home-buyer
life-guard
meeting-place
star-struck
post-code

Adjectives

Verbs

• **Write sentences using three words from each star to show their meanings.**

Now try this!

• **Make a chart to show how the words above are made up.**

Noun + noun	Noun + adjective	Adjective + adjective	Adjective + verb	Noun + verb	Verb + verb
life-guard	lead-free	red-handed	double-check	gift-wrap	spell-check

Teachers' note A chart like the one suggested in the extension activity could be displayed so that the children can add hyphenated words to it as they come across them.

Developing Literacy
Sentence Level Year 4
© A & C Black 1999

Air-blue and wave-whitened

Poets often make up hyphenated words.

• Write what you think these words mean.

Poet	Word	Meaning
John Betjeman	after-storm-lit	
Thomas Hardy	air-blue	
Brian Lee	Eden-green	
Gerard Manley Hopkins	Heaven-haven	
Christina Rossetti	leaf-crowned	
Thomas Hardy	years-deep dust	
William Shakespeare	pity-pleading eyes	
Kathleen Raine	memory-traces	
William Jay Smith	silver-scaled fish	
WB Yeats	wave-whitened	

Now try this!

• **Make a chart to show which types of words the poets' words are.**

• **Use each word in a sentence.**

Nouns	Adjectives

Teachers' note As a shared text, read a poem by one of the poets named; ask the children to listen for hyphenated words. They could make up some of their own and use them in their own poems.

Developing Literacy
Sentence Level Year 4
© A & C Black 1999

The owner's apostrophe

An apostrophe is used with a noun to show belonging.

 An apostrophe after a singular noun

Examples: Dad's car = the car owned by Dad
the girl's bike = the bike belonging to the girl
the town's market = the market of the town

• **Write captions for the pictures, using apostrophes.**

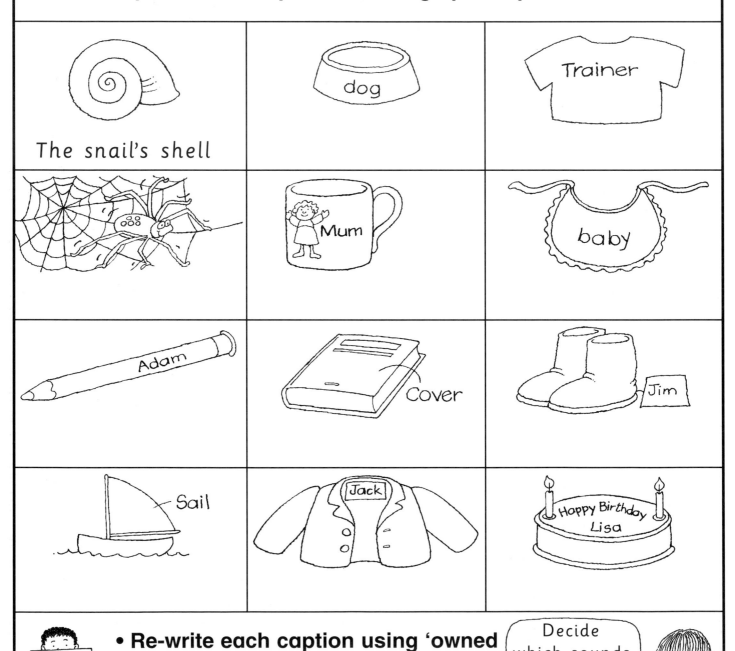

The snail's shell

dog

Trainer

Mum

baby

Adam

Cover

Jim

Sail

Jack

Happy Birthday Lisa

Now try this!

• **Re-write each caption using 'owned by', 'of' or 'belonging to'.**

Decide which sounds the best.

Teachers' note Stress that apostrophes are only used to show ownership with nouns. Ask the children if they can think of other words which show ownership (possessive pronouns). Remind them never to use an apostrophe in its, theirs, ours, yours or hers.

Developing Literacy
Sentence Level Year 4
© A & C Black 1999

Apostrophes in titles

• **Put the apostrophes into these book titles.**

The Emperors New Clothes

Carries War

The Pardoners Tale

Alices Adventures in Wonderland

Toms Midnight Garden

Harry Potter and the Philosophers Stone

Mr Wolfs Week

Joe Giants Missing Boot

Rosies walk

Bills New Frock

Osas Pride

Gullivers Travels

A Childs Garden of Verses

Old Possums Book of Practical Cats

Jessy and the Bridesmaids Dress

The Pilgrims Progress

Delias How to Cook Book

Ninnys Boat

A Midsummer Nights Dream

Charlottes Web

• **Make a chart to show who or what is owned in each title, and who or what owns it.**

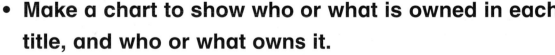

Title	What is owned?	Who owns it or who is it for?
The Emperor's New Clothes	new clothes	the emperor

Teachers' note The children could also re-write the titles using 'of', 'for' 'belonging to', 'owned by' and 'point of view' (whichever makes the best sense): for example, 'The War from Carrie's Point of View' and 'The Tale of the Pardoner'.

Developing Literacy
Sentence Level Year 4
© A & C Black 1999

The owners' apostrophes

An apostrophe to show ownership of a plural noun goes **after** the s.

An apostrophe after a plural noun.

• **Re-write these using apostrophes:**

the cloakroom for ladies
_____

the toilet for boys
_____

the tails of the cats
_____

the house belonging to the Browns
_____

the books owned by her parents
_____

the work of the pupils
_____

 Exceptions

In some plurals the apostrophe goes before the s.

These are plurals which do **not** end with s.

• **Learn these:**

| women's | men's | children's | mice's |

• **Add the apostrophes to these:**

the childrens library, the mices tails, the womens names, the mens addresses, the oxens stalls, the sheeps field, the geeses beaks, the peoples lives.

Now try this!

• **Make everything in these sentences plural.**

1. It was a man's shoe.

2. I found the girl's book.

3. The dog's bone was in the garden.

4. The fox stole the goose's egg.

5. He went to his friend's party.

6. A cow's horn appeared above the hedge.

Teachers' note The children should first complete pages 48 and 49. Ask them to describe the differences between the possessive forms of plurals and of singulars. In the extension activity, discuss changes which might be needed to the verbs.

Developing Literacy
Sentence Level Year 4
© A & C Black 1999

Contractions 1

When words are joined together, letters are sometimes missed out. This is called a <u>contraction</u>.

An apostrophe shows where the letters are missed out.

Examples: | do not = don't | | we have = we've |

- Write the contraction on each concertina.
- Write the missing letter on each note.

- Write these contractions in full:

I'm _____   I've _____   she's _____

they've _____   hadn't _____   couldn't _____

weren't _____   let's _____   he'll _____

I'll _____   can't _____   needn't _____

 Now try this! • **Write six sentences which contain contractions.**

Teachers' note The children could also list other contractions (and their long forms), saying which letters are omitted.

Developing Literacy
Sentence Level Year 4
© A & C Black 1999

51

Contractions 2

The following words are often contracted:

is	's	has	's	had	'd	have	've	not	n't
are	're	will	'll	would	'd	of	o'		

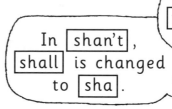

• **Re-write the sentences, using contractions.**

1. They will not play with us.

_____

2. I did not think we would arrive until two of the clock.

_____

3. We shall not be able to go to the party.

_____

4. Ian is going to Spain; he can not get a flight to France.

_____

5. You need not go if you do not want to.

_____

6. Do not worry about the broken cup — it does not matter.

_____

7. They are going to their gran's house if they have time.

_____

• **Make a list of phrases which contain** o' **, meaning** of **.**

Use a dictionary of phrases.

Teachers' note The children should first complete page 51. They could share their answers and say which letters have been omitted and/or changed in each example.

**Developing Literacy
Sentence Level Year 4
© A & C Black 1999**

What did they say?

- **Re-write the jokes using speech marks to show who asked and answered them.**

Useful words
announced
answered
asked
cried
muttered
replied
responded
said
shouted
whispered

What do you call a polar bear in the jungle?

Lost!

"What do you call a polar bear in the jungle?" asked the lion.
"Lost!" replied the elephant.

What happens when ducks fly upside-down?

They quack up!

_____

_____

_____

What did the scarf say to the hat?

I'll hang around — you go on ahead!

Ben

Sue

_____

_____

Now try this!

- **Re-write these jokes as if two people you know were telling them. Use speech marks and other punctuation.**
  1. Knock knock whos there Marietta Marietta who Marietta whole loaf
  2. Knock knock whos there Desi Desi who Desi take sugar

Teachers' note Using a shared text, revise the positions of punctuation marks in relation to speech marks: commas follow 'said', 'asked' and so on before speech, and punctuation marks at the end of speech are enclosed within the speech marks.

**Developing Literacy
Sentence Level Year 4
© A & C Black 1999**

The same but different

- **Match the sentences which have the same meaning.**
- **Write your answers on the chart.**

1	
2	
3	
4	
5	

1. Jack has not got any pencils.

2. Tara has a dog and so has May.

3. I have never been to Japan and neither have you.

4. We live in a flat and so we can not have a dog.

5. They had dinner and then they went out.

a) Neither of us has been to Japan.

d) Both Tara and May have dogs.

b) Because we live in a flat we can not have a dog.

c) Jack has no pencils.

e) After dinner they went out.

- **Write these sentences differently, but keep the same meanings.**

1. He found the parcel behind a bush and it was in a big black bag and he was surprised.

He was surprised to find _____

_____

2. Jill has no money and I have not got any either.

Neither _____

3. Chloe has a cat and Faye has too and Faye has a fish.

Both Chloe and Faye _____ ; Faye also _____

_____

- **Re-write and improve a piece of your own work in the same way.**

Teachers' note The children could make a note of the alternatives which they are likely to meet often: for example, 'has no' for 'has not got any', 'both...and...have' for '...has and so has...' and 'neither...nor...has' for '...has not and neither has...'

Developing Literacy Sentence Level Year 4 © A & C Black 1999

Positive and negative

- **Read the positive and negative sentences.**
- **Complete the chart.**

Remember the full stops and question marks.

Positive	Negative
Sarah collects stamps.	Sarah does not collect stamps.
He always wears a blue tie.	He never wears a blue tie.
I like crisps.	
Please park here.	
Should I write to him?	
That is my book.	
We often go to the park.	
	Kevin does not go to school.
	Mr Green can not drive.
	They have no car.
	This road is not suitable for heavy vehicles.
Visitors should leave their bags in the cloakroom.	
	Doesn't he want his tea?
	Can't you swim?

- **Copy a passage from a book, making all the positive sentences negative and all the negative sentences positive.**

Teachers' note Read the first two examples with the children and ask them to describe the changes which have been made; they should notice changes in word-order, changes to the words themselves and the addition or deletion of words.

Developing Literacy
Sentence Level Year 4
© A & C Black 1999

Statements and questions

This is a statement: | Tom is writing. |

It can be turned into a question: | Is Tom writing? |

• **Describe how it was changed.** _____

_____

• **Change these statements into questions.**

The baby's name is Jake.

This is the new shop.

The class has a new teacher.

The train is in the station.

Christmas Day is on the 25th of December.

You saw the old man asleep in his chair.

Ali can swim.

The pigeon flew home.

Mia left her coat at home.

Now try this!

• **Describe how you changed each statement to make it into a question.**

Think about punctuation, word-order and changed words.

Teachers' note There is often more than one way to make a statement into a question; the children can share their ideas.

56

Developing Literacy
Sentence Level Year 4
© A & C Black 1999

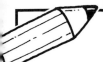

That's an order!

A statement can be changed into an order or command:

| You may sit here. | ➡ | Sit here. |

 'You may' has been taken away.

• **Change these statements to orders.**

I wish you would be quiet.

I would like you to give me a pencil.

You can change your money here.

I wish you would tell me your name.

You should leave your muddy boots at the door.

You must not play ball games here.

Drivers should keep to the left.

You can buy your ticket here.

We do not want you to walk on the grass.

I hope you have a nice day.

 Now try this!

• **Write six orders or commands for a partner to change into statements.**

Teachers' note The children could also identify statements and orders in a shared text and describe their purposes. They could explore the effects of changing them from one form to the other.

Developing Literacy
Sentence Level Year 4
© A & C Black 1999

Silly sentences

If you change the order of the words in a sentence it might not make sense.

Example: The mouse ran up the clock.

The clock ran up the mouse.

• **Turn this text into a silly story by swapping the nouns in each sentence.**

The first one has been done for you.

Alice went for a walk in the countryside.

The countryside went for a walk in Alice.

On the way she saw a man washing a car.

_____

Mrs Jones was looking out for the bus.

_____

Alice turned into the lane.

_____

A hare ran across the road.

_____

A horse looked over the fence.

_____

The farmers were herding the cows.

_____

Now try this!

• **Write six sentences which have words in the wrong order.**
• **Give them to a partner to sort out.**

Teachers' note The children could also write 'silly stories' (using sentences whose words are in the wrong order but are grammatically correct) which they could then change to make them more sensible.

Developing Literacy
Sentence Level Year 4
© A & C Black 1999

- **Sometimes a sentence makes sense when the order of the words is changed, but the sentence has a different meaning.**

| I mean what I say. | → | I say what I mean. |

- **Cut out the sentences and spread them out, face down.**
- **Take turns to turn over two sentences.**
- **If they are a pair, keep them.**
- **The winner is the player with the most pairs.**

I see what I eat.	I eat what I see.
I mean what I say.	I say what I mean.
He laughs when he runs.	He runs when he laughs.
I know what I am doing.	I am doing what I know.
I breathe when I sleep.	I sleep when I breathe.
He does what he is told.	He is told what he does.
I get what I like.	I like what I get.

Teachers' note Use this with page 60. Photocopy both pages on to card and, to allow re-use, laminate them before the children cut them out. Continued on page 60.

Developing Literacy
Sentence Level Year 4
© A & C Black 1999

Sentence pairs: sentence cards

Whistle while you work.	Work while you whistle.
Sing as you go.	Go as you sing.
He rings the changes.	He changes the rings.
She answered the questions.	She questioned the answers.
Pay as you earn.	Earn as you pay.
Buy now, pay later.	Pay now, buy later.
I eat to live.	I live to eat.
He reads to learn.	He learns to read.
He shouts orders.	He orders shouts.
She kneels when she prays.	She prays when she kneels.
They drive to work.	They work to drive.
I go where I like.	I like where I go.

Teachers' note (Continued from page 59.) During the plenary session the children could explain the meaning of each of the sentences in a pair. They could make additional sentence cards.

Developing Literacy
Sentence Level Year 4
© A & C Black 1999

An argument

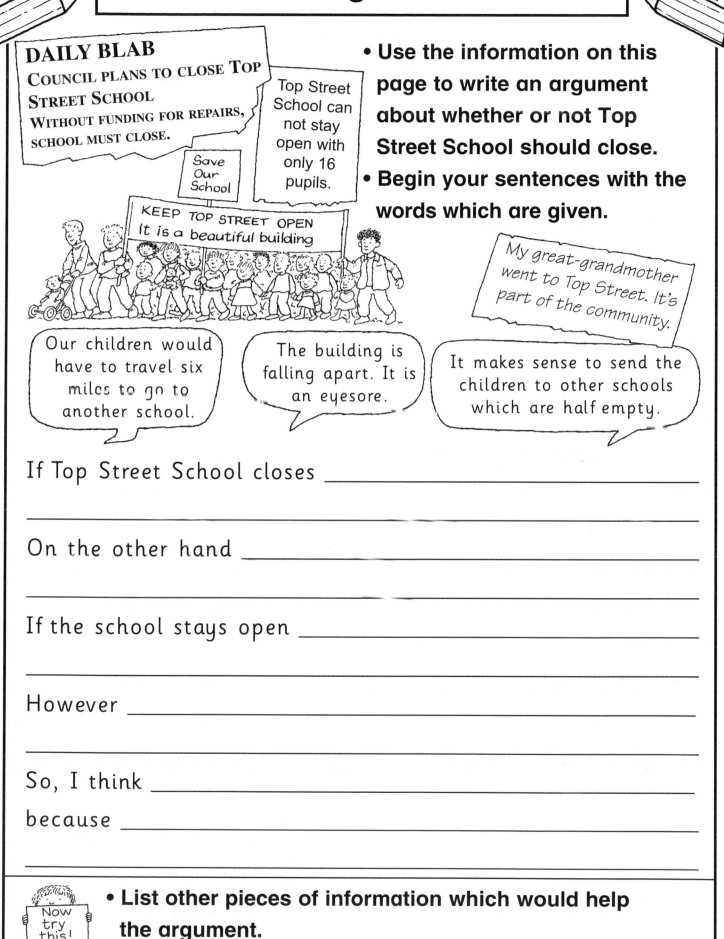

DAILY BLAB
COUNCIL PLANS TO CLOSE TOP STREET SCHOOL
WITHOUT FUNDING FOR REPAIRS, SCHOOL MUST CLOSE.

Top Street School can not stay open with only 16 pupils.

Save Our School

KEEP TOP STREET OPEN
It is a beautiful building

• **Use the information on this page to write an argument about whether or not Top Street School should close.**

• **Begin your sentences with the words which are given.**

My great-grandmother went to Top Street. It's part of the community.

Our children would have to travel six miles to go to another school.

The building is falling apart. It is an eyesore.

It makes sense to send the children to other schools which are half empty.

If Top Street School closes _____

_____

On the other hand _____

_____

If the school stays open _____

_____

However _____

_____

So, I think _____

because _____

Now try this!

• **List other pieces of information which would help the argument.**

Teachers' note The result of this activity is the outline of an argument, which the children could use as the basis for a more substantial one which is linked with text-level work on paragraphs and genre.

Developing Literacy
Sentence Level Year 4
© A & C Black 1999

Agreement

The <u>subject</u> of a verb is the person or thing which does the action.

- Change the verbs so that they agree with their subjects.

A Roman soldier in Britain writes home to his mum.

One has been done for you.

It b̶e̶ (is) very cold here, but the hard work keep me warm. The Britons knows how to keep warm. They wears warm clothes made from thick, woven cloth.

There is no cities here, so we has to build them. We be building roads too. I has been working on Watling Street. We has just laid a section of stone blocks. It settle nicely on the gravel which we lay yesterday. Marcus have all the luck. He are working in Camulodunum — they has lovely oysters there.

I has had news from Camulodunum. The Britons has sacked the city. Their leader are a fierce red-haired woman names Boudica. I hopes she do not come this way.

Now try this!

- **Make a chart on which to list the corrected verbs and their subjects.**

Verb	Subject
is	it
keeps	work

Teachers' note In a shared text, ask the children to identify the verbs and their subjects. They could also say how the verb would need to change if it had a different subject.

Developing Literacy Sentence Level Year 4 © A & C Black 1999

Proof-reading 1

- **Proof-read and correct this report.**
- **Use a red pen.**
- **Use the proof-reading marks.**
- **Write them in the margin as well as marking the mistake. The first two lines have been done for you.**

Proof-reading marks

∧	insert a letter or word.
⌒ and cross out the letter or word	Take out a letter or word.
⊗	Put a full stop.

∧n ∧g

⌒ ⊗

Testig magnets for strenth

We put a pine at the end of the ruler Then we tryed each magnet We started them at on 30cm and an movd them nerer to the pin We lookt to sea if the pin moovd and rote how many centimets away it was were

magnet

pin
ruler

we wold now which was were the strangest magnet It wold moove the pin from the longest distanse

- **Compare your proof-reading with that of a partner.**
- **Find other ways to improve the report.**
- **Re-write it.**

Now try this!

Teachers' note The children could first practise the three proof-reading marks which are introduced. Use them when marking their work.

Developing Literacy Sentence Level Year 4 © A & C Black 1999

63

Proof-reading 2

- **Proof-read and correct this passage.**
- **Write the proof-reading marks in the margin as well as marking the mistake.**

Use the proof-reading marks shown on page 63 as well.

The first two lines have been done for you.

Leonardo da Vinci was Born in italy in a village called vinci

Leonardo loved birdes He used to By them to set them free.

On day leonardo found a cave in.
he thought there migt be Something
intersting in it wich he could draw.
he wanted to go in, but he was scared.
He took a deep breathe and went in. It
was dark He coud not see anythig

- **Write a correct version of the above text.**

Teachers' note The children should first complete page 63. Encourage them to use the proof-reading marks for neatness when editing and proof-reading their own work.

Developing Literacy
Sentence Level Year 4
© A & C Black 1999